ANTHOLOGY OF POETRY
BY
YOUNG AMERICANS®

1997 EDITION
VOLUME CXLVII

Published by Anthology of Poetry, Inc.

©*Anthology of Poetry by Young Americans*®
1997 Edition
Volume CXLVII
All Rights Reserved©

Printed in the United States of America

To submit poems
for consideration in the 1998 edition of the
Anthology of Poetry by Young Americans®,
send to:

       Anthology of Poetry, Inc.
       PO Box 698
       Asheboro, NC 27204-0698

Authors responsible
for originality of poems submitted.

The Anthology of Poetry, Inc.
307 East Salisbury • P.O. Box 698
Asheboro, NC   27204-0698

ISBN: 1-883931-09-6

Anthology of Poetry by Young Americans®
is a registered trademark of
Anthology of Poetry, Inc.

The Poetry in our anthology may rhyme, but it doesn't have to. It may have rhythm, but it doesn't have to. It may follow a particular form, but it doesn't have to. It may have punctuation, capital letters and stanzas, but it doesn't have to. The only boundaries this poetry has is the imagination of our young gifted authors. We selected these poems from submissions from all over the country and hope you enjoy them as much as we have. We tried to present the poems as the author wrote them, in their format and punctuation. We would like to extend a special thanks to all the poets who participated. We are expecting great things from them in the future.

The Editors

MY DOG BO

I have a dog his name is Bo
he likes to lick my mom's toe
He sleeps with me in my bed
when I wake up he's on my head.

Eric J. Beyer
Age: 10

SCHOOL

We listen to the teacher well,
We listen for the bell,
We listen when she reads to us,
But we don't when she yells!

Ashley Frantzen
Age: 9

AN OLD FRIEND

He was like a flawless friend,
  like a dress with not one mend.
Sitting on the old green bench,
  is a memory not in French.
My love to him means oh, so much,
  I pray to him to keep in touch.
Yet we all know what it's like,
  to be alone on life's big hike.
His love for me is more than strong,
  than life alone that's so, so long.
He was my best and greatest friend,
  I'll love him back until the end.

In Remembrance of Carl Hendrickson

Jeanne Czipri
Age: 11

CARS AND MARS

I would not like to go to Mars,
because they don't have any cars.
Spaceships can fly, so they must not be heavy,
but I'd rather drive a '57 Chevy

Timothy Keefe
Age: 9

NATURE

I'm a nature poet
Standing on the rays
of the sun.

Writing nature, sun
Poems

My poems shine down
like God does on
Earth,
Sun,
on waters of the sea,

Always and forever

Mallory Ness

NAMELESS PAPER

I am a nameless paper.
You write on me,
You color on me,
You draw on me,
But you never care
Enough about me
To put your name on me.

Desiree Dunham
Age: 11

3

WATHCHAMACALLIT

Far away there's a planet called
Watchamacallit.
The year is 4000 B.C.
Time goes backwards there,
you know
And it is hard to see.

The people there, they have
green skin
And a fair amount of warts, too.
The ocean is bright, the sky
so gray,
And the people there wish they were
blue.

Sometimes when they worry,
They often get sick
And this makes them worry
some more.
They worry why bears are as nice as
the kittens.
The doctors there can't find a
cure.

When they go to sleep,
they lie on their
heads
And this does make them so
dizzy.
And when they wake up

In the morning so bright
They're all over again in a
tizzy.

Lorna Riggle
Age: 11

THE PANTHER

The panther is like a leopard
Except it hasn't been peppered.
Should you behold the panther crouch,
Be prepared to say "OUCH!"
Better yet, if called by a panther
It is best, not to answer.

Matthew Wolding
Age: 12

ANIMALS

I love to watch baby birds fly,
And watch the rabbits hop on by.
I love to see white-tailed deer,
And squirrels hiding nuts so near!

Sarah Bock
Age: 9

5

MOONLIGHT

In the darkness of night
I sit here and stare at the pale moonlight.
The moon casting shadows on the darkness.
They dance in the silence of the darkness.
The stars shine on the shadows,
Putting them in an endless battle.
As the stars fall across the empty sky,
We know soon they shall die.
A cool breeze blows across the land,
Together they walk hand and hand.
In the darkness of night
I sit here and stare at the pale moonlight.

Nestor S. Martinez

THANKSGIVING

The leaves fall down,
around, and 'round.
I smell the turkey,
it's bound to be found.
The leaves are turning
green and brown.
The turkey is still bound
to be found.
The leaves are floating
all downtown.
The turkey is still bound
to be found.

Christopher Cope

THE HAUNTED HOUSE

haunted house
haunted house
what's inside
no one knows
not even a mouse
goblins and ghouls
know what's inside
what's inside is
bats, ghouls, and
spiders and witches
that's what's inside.

Garrett J. Will
Age: 10

MOM

Whenever I need help,
I just yell, "Mom."
I yell when I am scared.
I yell when I am mad.
I yell when I am sad.
When I need her
There she will be,
Happy as can be, just for me.

Christina Mendoza
Age: 11

MY THINGS TO DO

Tonight I had soccer,
Plus lots of homework to do,
I had to wash the dishes,
Now I'm finally through.

Laura Schaffer
Age: 9

SUMMER

In the summer I hum.
In the summer I tummer on the drum.
In the summer I hear sweet songs
As I go down the road.
Is it a toad?

Katie Fowler
Age: 9

MORNING FISHING

Early morning on the dock
With my little chair,
I see the morning birds
Walking with great care.
I throw my line out in the lake,
And watch the bobber as it shakes.
Then I see a little fish swimming by my line,
I know that it will taste, "Mighty fine."
When I see the bobber sink
I get excited it's hard to think.
I take my catch off the hook
And run to give all a look.

Nick Motyka
Age: 9

THE PET

My pet Simba jumps on to my bed
licks my face, nose, and head
when I go to sleep he purrs in my ear,
then I know I have nothing to fear.
So now you can see
why my cat loves me.

Timothy DeSimone
Age: 9

HALLOWEEN

Halloween is full of scary things,
it is full of ghosts and goblins,
it has witches and black cats,
there is jack-o'-lantern's and witches' stew.

Sarah Vlakancic
Age: 9

LOVE

Love is tender, love is kind.
It occupies the heart and mind.

Love fills up an empty soul,
And makes a broken heart seem whole.

Love is tender, faithfully true,
It binds together I and you.

Love is in each baby's birth,
Yet reaches all the ends of earth.

And even if the mountains quake,
And the hills and valleys shake...

Love will stand, for love is strong.
Love is everlasting long.

Erica Ruddy

FRIENDS

I like my friends,
we ride our bikes from end-to-end.
We stay together, we play together,
we never end without each other.
We play 'til eight,
then we say it's too late,
so we say bye-bye
for the night.

Holly Pasieka
Age: 9

THE SNOW WALK

When I walk through the
soft, white, cold snow,
my boots make the snow crunch.

The soft snow is like a blanket
covering the brown grass.

The green, spiky pine trees are soft now,
and the bushes are like popcorn balls.

The breeze swipes through the cold, frosty air,
giving us all a chill.

Taryn Gabbert
Age: 8

MOMMY

I love my mommy.
She gives me hugs and kisses.
When I need them most.

Cheryl L. Okuda
Age: 6

D olphins live
O n
N eptune.
A ll of them eat
L asagna. The
D olphins swim in swimming pools.

Don O'Brien
Age: 9

BASKETBALL

Jim is my name
and basketball is my game.
I shoot with the best
and steal from the rest.
I block when I'm hot
and I rebound when I'm not.

Jim Schroeder
Age: 10

DUCK

He is calling to
His yellow family, "Quack!"
"Quack!" in the blue pond.

Daniel Hankes
Age: 5

GIRAFFE

Inside the zoo my
Long-necked friend reaches up to
Eat leaves off a tree.

Krystina Johnson
Age: 5

WINTER

Snow is falling,
the cold wind calling.
The tree stands bare,
which I love to stare.
And when I play in the snow,
all I can say is whoa!

Kelly Helene Westrom
Age: 9

Slavery
cruel, harsh
whipping, farming, cotton picking
plantation, masters, Lincoln, underground railroad
voting, educating, owning
humane, easy
Freedom

Christopher Okuda
Age: 12

COW

My cow makes milk and
Is black and white. She say, "Moo,
Moo," and eats grass, too.

Jeff Slehofer
Age: 6

DRAGONS

Fire dragons live
Forever in caves under
The sea and play tag.

Kurt Porzelt
Age: 5

HOMEWORK HOMEWORK

H omework can be fun, but why,
O h, why do we have so much homework? Why do
   we have so
M uch sometimes? That's when I get mad. If you
E at and do homework at the same time, you might spill
W ater on it and I'll keep saying why,
O h, why do we have so much homework? I
R eally want to know why we have so much homework
   even my
K itty gets tired of watching me sit and do homework!!

H omework can be a pain in the neck. I would much
   rather be playing
O utside on
M y trampoline. I don't like homework
E specially English homework. I like it
W hen it's fun like coloring a graph
O r even just
R eading but not the
K nowledge rating vocabulary sheets for reading.
   Sometimes I like homework but sometimes I don't!!

Marissa Hill
Age: 11

NATURAL MUSIC

The leaves fall in rhythm,
The birds sing in unison.

The wind whispers softly,
The river flows with the softest grace.

The crickets twing their beautiful notes,
While the waterfall sounds the applause!

Beth Petrenko
Age: 12

LITTLE ITALY

Italy that little Italian boot.
The gondolas sailing in Sicily.
The red hot chili peppers so hot, the food so good.
Those Italians hard at work.
I love the Italian boot.

Katie Pintozzi
Age: 9

MY FAITHFUL FRIEND

He was waiting for me at the door when my parents
Brought me home from the hospital.
He liked sitting by my crib while I took my naps.
He was there when my mom fed me.
He didn't seem to mind all my crying and fussing.
He sat by the window and watched me
Walk off to school.
He was always there for me when I returned
At the end of the day.
He was never too sick or too tired to play with me.
He would stay by my side when I wasn't feeling good.
He was gentle and loving.
He wouldn't harm a fly.
He got old like we all will do someday.
He got sick and had to be put to sleep.
He seemed to understand that it was time
For him to go.
He went quietly and peacefully
Just like we all knew he would.
He will always have a special place in my heart.
He was my dog, Shaggy.
He was and is my faithful friend.

Laura Davis
Age: 11

Inside of me there lies
A never-ending snowmobile trip
Trying to take me to the limits of the earth
The ultimate adventure waiting to break through
Trying to launch me to extraordinary heights
Flying down frozen highways at a suicidal rate
Inside of me there lies
A snowmobile that doesn't break

Andy Maxwell
Age: 13

DOGS

D ogs are cozy and also one
O f my favorite animals. They're fun to play with
 and I want to
G et a dog, but my parents said we can't.
 My brother wants one so badly.
S ometimes we go over to our neighbor's house
 and play with their dog.
 Sometimes we give him water and snacks;
 his name is Barkus; a real fun and wild beagle.
I LOVE DOGS!!!!

Amanda Riccio
Age: 11

THE BLIZZARD

Ho, ho, ho,
Santa's coming in the snow
If he does that's a fright
What if there's a blizzard in sight
Oh now what if Santa gets hurt
Or maybe there's flying dirt
Maybe he's out of fright
But there's still
The blizzard in sight.

Matt McAllister
Age: 10

MY PUPIL

When it does not rain
my pupil loses her brain
which is almost everyday.
She eats hay
for lunch at school
and drinks drool.
But when it rains
it's like she has two brains.
Her parents say it's because
she wants to sell flood insurance.

Jill J. Parikh
Age: 9

HALLOWEEN NIGHT

On Halloween night the children dress up
as witches, goblins, ghosts and other stuff.
They are very scary children.
They go trick-or-treating on Halloween night
and scare all the people with a very big fright!!

Meghan Riley
Age: 8

SAMANTHA

A cat who's mixed up
She licks me when I'm sleeping.
I like her a lot.

Amielia Gonzalez
Age: 5

BUNNY

Bunny has sharp teeth
He eats carrots and lettuce
He's soft and cuddly.

Megan Hand
Age: 5

THE WORLD HAS ENDED

The world has ended
it's a horrible day
the sun has gone
the cloud's here to stay
the world has ended
it's all going downhill
there's a big empty space
which nothing will fill

Shoshana Blumenthal
Age: 13

IN MY DREAMS

In my dreams,
I travel beyond where man can go.
Places so exotic, they are surrounded by glassy domes.
Fish amble by,
They wear midnight black suits,
With coal black top hats.
Their brides wear cream white dresses.
Felines roam the town,
Wearing flashy, ruby bow ties.
Birds soar through the sky,
Like a leaf, floating in the autumn air.
In my dreams.

Anthony Lopez
Age: 14

WINTER

The snow fell softly around me
Such a beautiful sight to see
My feet crunching with each step
A sound in my ear I kept

Kristan Catalani
Age: 13

RIBBONS

He curls up on top
Wakes me up and jumps off quick.
I love him very much.

Emily LoCicero
Age: 5

DOLPHINS

They play in the water
Flipping and jumping up high.
Waving good-bye!

Gina Lukasik
Age: 5

CHANGING SEASONS

The colorful leaves fall to the ground,
The ground turns fluffy and white,
When the snow melts, the kids frown,
But soon rejoice that the weather is right.

Colleen Mottram
Age: 12

DOLPHIN

They bounce balls in air
Jumping and waving at me
Splashing and squeaking.

Thomas B. Miller
Age: 5

CHIP

He nibbles on nuts
Chases me around everywhere
And sleeps in my hat.

Kevin Sinnott
Age: 5

SKIING

All the snow around
Feel the wind in your face
Zooming by and dodging trees
The cold makes you sneeze
If you go too high you may get nauseous
Pine trees all around but
They don't make a sound
Hot cocoa in the lodge
Sitting by the fireplace makes you warm
The lifts can get scary when you go really high
But thinking of good thoughts makes the fear go away
The trees, the mountains, and all the vast space
You may see these things as you face your fear
Going up and down the lifts
If you don't see the moguls they will make you fall
But if you are really good you can take them all
The thrill of speeding down a mountain
Feels like nothing I've experienced before

Jeremy Peake
Age: 11

BOOMER

Boomer is my dog
He licks me on my cheeks a lot.
I care for him alone.

Elizabeth Smith
Age: 5

24

HALLOWEEN

Trick-or-treat is coming
Run away from ghosts.
It is fun with costumes.
Come and join the host.
Know each other's costumes,
Or you'll be surprised.
It is really just your friends
Behind those spooky eyes!

Natalie Chan
Age: 6

I was in the Amazon,
when I saw a swan yawn.
I said my farewells in a few hours I was gone

When I got home I sent a fax to Jax
about a sax.
I sent that fax to Jax about the sax,
because the sax is big,
but as fragile as a twig.

After awhile I moved to the Nile,
and met Dr. Vile.
Dr. Vile told me to go back
to where I came from,
but I said "No," chewing a piece of gum.

Sean Michael Layton
Age: 10

ME

Me, me, me.
I am me.
I look like me.
I am me.
Me I am.
I am me --
The me I used to be.
Me, me, me.

Christina Delicata
Age: 6

MARK

M agic is fun.
A pples are something good.
R ecess is my best time.
K icking is my game.

K itty cocktails are good to drink.
O ceans are cool.
W aves are cool to go in.
A lligators are awesome.
L ike guards watching people.
I slands are fun to go on.
K ites are fun to fly.

Mark Kowalik
Age: 9

RELAX!

The morning is as fresh as new fallen snow.
The dew twinkles like little stars.
Ah, the smell of freshly cut grass!
I feel relaxed.

The sun is just rising over the trees,
Perfect white sand lying in wait,
The sun's rays sparkle on the water like fireworks:
I feel relaxed.

The shades of green are as peaceful to the eye
As the colorful chirping birds are calming to the ear.
I feel relaxed.

My clubs are gleaming like spokes on a wheel,
My shoes are shined,
And I don't have another line:
Golf: I feel RELAXED!

Robert Peter Grube
Age: 11

HERMIE

He swims in the bowl
Waiting for food to come down
Wishing for a friend.

Jeffrey Wilczynski
Age: 5

MEMORIES

I can remember all the good times
we have shared
From laughs to cries we have
always cared
A shoulder to cry on, a joke to
laugh at
From cookies and ice cream, to baseballs
and bats
At sleepovers we would play Truth
or Dare
You and I would make up one
great pair
From movies and pizza and shopping for
funny hats
To Halloween goblins, witches and old
black cats
Like a good loyal buddy, you've always
been willing to share
Giving advice and fixing
our hair
Friends we will be and never
will part
A friendship to last a whole lifetime and forever
in our hearts.

Michelle Mugnolo
Age: 11

TOYS, OH TOYS

Toys, oh toys, you are my friends,
You'll always be with me until the end,
You provide me with fun,
Until the day is done,
Toys, oh toys, you are my friends.

Legos are worthy,
But not very nerdy,
They are cool creations,
From people's imaginations.

Board games are my name,
They're in my Hall of Fame,
My favorite game is Clue,
I wonder if cases come true!

Challenging puzzles
Are worth the trouble,
'Cause brainstorming's a need,
But not an awful deed.

And last of all, there are video games,
If I don't have them, it's a pain,
The best one of all is N-Sixty Four,
I went to Toys 'R' Us, I was happy out
the door

William Seng Tan
Age: 10

THE RIDE

On a chopper with no doors,
Like the kind they use in wars.
Since it just had rained before,
I saw waterfalls galore!
Soaring through the open sky,
Feeling like I could fly.
Wow! The canyon is so deep,
And the mountains which are very steep.
By the time we were landing,
Encore! Encore! We were demanding.

Aalok Shah
Age: 10

MY RAINBOW BEAUTY

My rainbow doll, oh my rainbow colored doll,
Just sitting there,
With blondish hair,
On my dresser all alone,
Except for one thing, that's a comb,
With bright blue eyes,
Looking at me, in such a surprise,
My rainbow doll, oh my rainbow colored doll,
Sitting there looking so small,
My rainbow beauty is the most pretty of all.

Noreen Qazi
Age: 10

ODE TO MY LAVA LAMP

You shine so bright with your bright light
and your green colored goo,
  You look so cool with assorted colors
like red, purple, and blue.
  At first you just start to stand there,
looking and feeling hot,
  But then you start to come alive,
shoot up, bubble, and pop.
  With your wax that looks like lava,
people gawk and stare,
  To me I think you're popular,
to others they just don't care.
  Lava lamp, lava lamp, your colors
shine so bright,
  Too bad because at nine o'clock
I turn you out at night.

Eddie Manofsky
Age: 11

As I lie 'neath my window
I sense the black widow,
with eight legs and eight eyes,
watching me at my windowsill.
As I sense the creature near,
I began to fear.
It fell like a feather onto my hand.
It squeezes my vein and injects its venom.
Then I say Mommy!
The end,
Or is it?
Never know will we.

Bradley Enrici

JOE

There once was a man named Joe,
he racked his garden with a hoe.
He would work and work every day,
he was like a needle in hay.
He worked all day.
He worked all night.
He worked unless there was no light.
So if you see this man named Joe,
stop by and say "hello,"
but be careful he might hit you
with his hoe.

Mandy Letizia
Age: 11

THE TOY TAKER

Good-bye my bears,
My sweet little teddies,
And farewell my doll named Betty,
I wish you could stay and then we could play
Hide-and-seek,
Where's Little Bo Peep,
And I wish I could keep all of you.
My dog, my doll and my ghost that says boo!
But now, oh dear here he comes,
Here comes the toy taker to take you
Unless I pay the sums,
But no we are poor,
So out the door,
And to never ever be seen again.

They'll untie your strings and take out your stuffing,
But I couldn't let that happen to you,
I'd be huffing and puffing,
By that I mean that I would be worried to death,
About you and Beth.

But ah, that was only a dream,
So I get to keep my train that blows out steam.
So farewell little toy taker, we're knocking you down,
And pack up your bags you're leaving town.

Melinda Innocenti
Age: 10

SNOW

Snow, snow, you make my heart glow
the harder you fall, the more that I know
that...I can't wait to go out and play in the snow

Snow, snow, I like you a lot
I love to go outside to jump and to trot
I fall and I slip and I leap and I slide
and when I'm on ice, I just love to glide

Snow, snow, I watch you at night
I think to myself...what a beautiful sight
You fall to the ground
without making a sound
I'm excited to play and to roll all around

Snow, snow, you've melted away
I think to myself...why can't you stay?
just a little bit longer
oh please if you could
stay a little while longer, you know that you should

But...

Snow, snow, I hope that you know
that you will always make my heart glow

Corey Tallent
Age: 11

SEA SUNSETS

Have you ever watched a sunset,
while standing on the beach?

The great, golden ball
sets over the dark sea.

Orange and pink rays,
explode from the sun,
far into the sky.

Finally the sun goes,
far, far, far, below.
Into the deep
dark sea
it shall
go.

Allison Petrak
Age: 13

I WILL DO IT

I will do it
Yes I will, yes I will
Don't try to stop me

Larissa Espiritu
Age: 7

FREEDOM IS....

Freedom is...
the birds of the sky,
birds with no limit
to where they can fly.

Freedom is...
a starlit night;
a vastness before you,
a clear path of sight.

Freedom is...
the losing of chains;
to leave them behind,
to forget all the pains.

Freedom is...
the oceans and seas;
with endless direction,
go where you please.

Freedom is...
an unlocked door;
it must be opened,
for you to get more.

Freedom is...
the dawning light;
it starts out dim,
but through time becomes bright.

Freedom is...
the falling of rain,

it is something
all wish to obtain.

Freedom is...
all this and more,
it came to us
from a mighty roar.

"It is finished," he cried
when he died on the tree
Jesus Christ died,
so that all may be free.

Sam McCash
Age: 17

WISHING

When I wish upon a star
I wonder if all wishes go far
Then I think it must be true
That they'll go far in the sky of blue.
I like to wish almost every night
On stars burnt out from the moon's
bright light;
Stars so tiny, so fragile, and yet
they have a light that's ready and set
for wishing every night
Upon a star.

Rebecca Weber
Age: 10

Q

I'll never understand the capital letter Q
It looks just like the number 2
Maybe someday I'll begin to see
The difference between the two of these

Kathleen Rose O'Rourke
Age: 9

LIGHTNING

Lightning, a golden rope on which man cannot climb.
Lightning, a golden spear which man cannot grasp.
Lightning, nature's way of troubling mankind.

Lei Curtis
Age: 11

OSTRICH

She is large and has
long legs. She lays huge eggs and
Her name is Opal.

Megan Lawler
Age: 6

TO ME SPRING IS....

To me spring is soft cries of young
Flowers wildly dancing.
Leaves that just recently sprung,
and clouds have started their prancing.

To me spring is the sun kissing the earth.
Leaves awake from their long nap.
Butterflies play, fly, and wind surf.
And thunder starts to joyfully rap.

To me spring is rainbows painting the sky.
The cold starts to retire.
Pattering rain plays a lullaby.
And crickets sing in a choir.

To me spring is winds that gleefully sing.
Squirrels excitedly greet their tree.
There's a soft flutter of a bird's wing.
And that's what spring is to me!

Danielle Nicole Izac
Age: 12

THE SOUL

This is a spider soul speaking,
A spider lays in his cool bed, dead!
Something fell on his big head.
He didn't know what hit him,
He thought and thought and thought,
But he didn't know what hit him.
Oh, well, so what,
He's dead as a door nail.

Thomas Avram
Age: 8

HANSEL AND GRETEL

Through the woods to the witch's house,
Two children walked quiet as a mouse.
Nibbling, nibbling to their hearts content,
The witch came out all crooked and bent.
No one had ever seen a witch so mad,
Nor laid eyes on children so sorry and sad.
The children to become the witch's meal,
They plotted to avoid this vicious deal.
They pushed that witch into the oven so hot,
And out of the forest like a missile they shot.
A chest of gold ends the story,
between witches and children, no guts no glory.

Gia Jean Sullivan
Age: 10

THE HAUNTED HOUSE

I opened the door
and the floor creaked,
I looked at my friend,
she was really freaked.
We took some steps,
a strange noise came out,
I couldn't wait, I wanted to shout.
We heard something say,
"Who is there? Is it a bear?"
We scrambled away as fast as we could,
we ran and we ran,
into the woods.
At last we were safe, away from the house,
Who was that there?
Was it a mouse?
I will never go back,
not if I'm dared,
'cause I...was really scared.

Katie Dabkey
Age: 11

BUTTERFLY

Butterfly flutters
And lands on a flower in
My pretty garden.

Kelsey Maren Kovac
Age: 5

MONSTERS

Monsters are very, hairy and scary,
They will eat you because you're as small as a berry.
Monsters are mean and green,
Some are fat,
Some are lean,
But no monster I know was ever clean.

Kathleen Elizabeth O'Connor

AN OPEN DOOR IN THE SKY

One day I looked up in the sky,
I looked up in the sky so high.
Higher than the birds may soar,
I thought I saw an open door.
I looked inside, to my surprise
I saw a man who was old and wise.
He said I must use what I possess
To make myself a great success.
So when I'm grown I'll use his advice
To make my life a paradise.
Next time you go outside and play
On a clear and sunny day,
Look to the sky, and you will see
How that man enchanted me.

Nathan Yu
Age: 10

SPIDERS

A spider is a creepy thing.
They are fast, they are smart,
They have very fancy art.
They suck your blood,
They shoot poisonous venom,
They wrap you up in thread,
If you get enough spider bites,
Soon you will be dead!

David B. Barron
Age: 9

C reepy crawly
R uns fast
E agle eyes
E eek
P oison
Y ikes!!

S hoots silk
P aralyzes his prey
I nteresting
D racula type teeth
E xcellent
R are
S pins webs

Brooke Blazevich
Age: 9

S ly.
P laying ball.
I cky smelling.
D addy long legs.
E ats all kinds of bugs.
R unning to a haunted house!
S pook!

Peter Borman
Age: 8

WRITING MUSIC

When I write music it just flows to me
Like the wind upon my face,
Sometimes I may get a storm
Sometimes I am stuck in one place.

I like to write in a quite place
Like in a meadow or under a tree.
I look around me and see birds
Sometimes one, two or three.

I can hear the music in my head
And have someone play it,
It sounds so good
I think it will be a hit!

Anne Swenson

SPIDERS

Spiders are really, really fast.
They have a cephalothorax.
They are very creepy.
They can also be sneaky.
When I see them
I'll yell Ahhhh,
Because they are the creepiest thing
That I ever saw!

Christine Ritten
Age: 7

REMEMBER, TOGETHER

Remember the creatures whose lives are at stake
Remember the help that we all give or take
Remember that this is a planet of one
Remember the products we waste by the ton
Remember the hope, children look up to you
Remember someday they'll be role models too
Remember, together we can make the rain
    pure once again!
Remember, together, children, women, and men
Remember, together the planet can stay alive
Remember, together we can equally thrive

Sarah Suzuki
Age: 12

SPIDERS

Spiders are icky, picky, and tricky.
They're a blood sucking venomous icky
Picky sight!
They fight, they bite all night.
And they're not a pretty sight.

Joey Johnson
Age: 8

DREAMS

As I lie in my bed
I think and think with my head
of all the things I could do
here's some maybe ones for you.

I want to be an artist
or maybe tame a beast
go to the moon or throw a harpoon
or I could go to a lake to look at a loon.

I could be anything that I want to be
if my mind is right and clear enough to see
I can do it I know if I put my mind to it
I just hope I don't fall into "can't do it."

Shannon McGivney

TONIGHT IS THE NIGHT

Tonight is the night
Where the creepy things crawl
Where the venomous things
Intend to kill
Tonight is the night
Where the Dracula type things
Go and blood suck their prey
You better hope it will soon be day.

Tim Canino
Age: 8

HALLOWEEN HAS COME!

Halloween has come!
"Trick-or-treat" to get a treat.
Monsters, gobstoppers,
Kings, and queens,
Wizards and lizards,
Frogs, and hogs,
Grapes, and vines,
Cherries, and chimes,
Or Ghosts, or hosts,
That's what Halloween is all about,
"Trick-or-treat!" Halloween has come!

Kristina Thoryk
Age: 12

I know a spider who loves to glide,
To catch the prey which would be a fly.
This is a shamrock spider so he must be green!
The spider loves to eat bugs and shamrock
that grows in the beam
But when the green spider ate a shamrock
he disappeared out of sight!
The green spider never came back,
because he was out of sight!

Katherine Barg
Age: 8

MY BIRD

There was a little bird who flew so high each day
From tree to tree he flew
Singing a song so nice
He made a nest that was so new.

Up and up he went
Way up to the sky
I know he will not fall
I could not see him with my eye.

The bird was a cardinal
He was my pet
So red and so lovely
The prettiest bird yet.

Krystin Conboy

CALVIN DROOLS

Calvin and Hobbes were very cool.
But they quit so I think they drool.

That's my opinion, you must not think I'm a fool.
I used to think they ruled.

I just don't like 'em now because they're quitters.
They're worse than my old baby-sitters.

Hobbes and Calvin are plain old critters.

John C. Garza
Age: 11

LOVE

Love is kindness,
love is tenderness.

Love is sharing,
love is caring.

Love is powerful,
love is wonderful.

Love is the glue,
that makes life smooth.

Rebekah Bakewicz
Age: 11

PORK

Pork purrs and likes food.
He plays with a ball of yarn.
Dogs are not his friends.

Michael Acosta
Age: 5

My favorite place in LaGrange is my basement
because my room is in it.
I like it because it has a TV, computer,
and my own bathroom in it.
I have my own closet.
My closet has my TV in it.

Angelo Christophell
Age: 8

I think spiders are very sly.
Sometimes they even die.
Then they quickly creep without a peep.
They crawl up a tree and slip and fall right on me.
If they bite you, I bet you will yell E-E-E-.
And you better skedaddle!

Anna Fina Friel
Age: 8

PRAIRIE

The smell of the fresh brisk morning air,
Opened my sleeping eyes.
The soft rumble of the distant buffalo soothed me.
The wise eyes of the owl judged me from afar
The tall grass danced with the light breeze,
Back and forth,
Back and forth.

Shannon Hilligoss
Age: 12

S harp fangs
H airy legs
A mazing
M ean, green bug-eating machine
R iding on webs
O oooowwwww
C reepy
K illing insects

Sneaky
P laying
I cky
D ying
E agle eye
R unning fast

Mike Konrad

BORN THIS WAY

sun spreads glitter over the barrio
people wake, talk, sing
their words clicking and whirring foreignly
faces shadowed and charcoal hair
names of Garcia and Gonzales and Perez
reflections of life
   they are mexican

warming smells of tortillas
laughing voices of brown-haired children
sticks swinging at papered pinatas
   texas

hungry voices crying out
disordered lives thrown together
so many mixed as if the same

hair too dark, faces too dark
young boys run in the shadows
knives and guns flashing
a culture falling,

a woman walks
sun falling onto her fair hair
with a child of dark curls and a smile lighting her face

the sun reflects dancing images off store windows
the woman leans down
for this child there will be no entrance here

The little girl's eyes are clouded now
they move again
heat waves on the pavement

this time a new destination
but denied entrance again
more people turning their faces away
saying without words her worth is not enough
the little girl stands outside looking in on a place
she may never know
in a world that holds no expectations

so where
does a little girl go
with no way out
does she seek for dreams
too far away to reach -- a star's distance

only time knows the answer

Katherine Ann Unmuth
Age: 15

BELIEVE

We cannot see God
But we know that he is there
Living in others

Emily Zielinski
Age: 12

CHORUS

A boy running through the forest
How softly he cries
He hears an exhilarating chorus
That sadness finally dies

James Bowers
Age: 13

RAIN

The rain comes down hard,
Drip, drip, drip, on the window,
Will it ever stop?

Colleen Kmak
Age: 12

A LEAP IN LIFE

Stretching for the sky,
Taking a big leap in life,
The hawk begins flight.

Matthew Eckstein
Age: 13

BABY BUFFALO

Watch the prairie grasses standing TALL, waving
like the wind in the rustling trees.
As I walk,
I can taste the fresh gulps of air
  that pop into my mouth.

                                    up
Smell the purple violets springing   just like
  weeds in the grass,
    and taste their spray of freshness
as it passes by.

Listen to the crushed leaves as we squash them
                under our hooves.
                But,
alas, listen to the rumble of the earthquake as
we run.

Feel the rippling muscles pass me by,
as we run,
looking like a herd of brown mountains.

                              Nicholette Marie Andrews

THE SEA

Reaching for the sky,
while spreading out its branches,
a tree begins to grow.

                              Jenna R. Leone
                              Age: 12

GLOOMY

A bad gloomy day
With rain against the
Window
It will never stop

Erin Lindsey
Age: 12

MOUNTAINS

Huge masses of rock
They slope into the blue sky
Towering above.

Katie Kula
Age: 12

Michael Jordan
Tall, quick
Shoots, dribbles, scores
A real champ!
Athlete

Owen Costello
Age: 12

Jesus
Holy, forgiving
Praying, healing, caring
He walks with us through hard times.
Savior

Jenn Wodzinski
Age: 13

CLOUD

A cloud in the sky.
It's menacing when angry.
But cries when upset.

Rachel LeClercq
Age: 13

PETALS

A blooming flower.
Gleaming petals in the sun.
Bees will be coming.

Meghan Long
Age: 13

Leaves
Colorful light
Falling twirling dancing
Leaves surrounding my yard.
Golden feathers

Christina Mulka
Age: 13

LIGHTNING

Flashing suddenly,
Disappearing just as fast,
And then it is gone.

Kevin M. Bailey
Age: 12

Ocean
Calm, beautiful
Relaxing, swimming, sailing
The waves crash down over the rocks.
Sea

Mike DiCristina
Age: 12

Turkeys
gobble, wild
carving, cooking, stuffing
hungry, yummy, anxious, excited
Turkeys

John T. Kobylarz
Age: 10

River
long wide
trickling falling running
rivers climb and fall
Stream

Mike Litwicki
Age: 12

YELLOW

Yellow is my favorite color,
It shines up all the world.
It is as bright as the new morn' sun,
That shines upon the daisies and buttercups.

Amy Lynn Gregerson

SNAKES

They sliver around
Frightening and scaring all!
Making an S in the sand.

Patrick Mortimer
Age: 5

WINTER

Winter comes and winter's cold.
Winter comes and it brings snow.
It freezes water, strips the trees,
It's very cold, and shakes the knees.
When you come home you do the polka
And you drink some real hot coca (cocoa).
Looking out your window real high,
You feel like you could touch the sky.
Winter comes and winter's cold.
Winter comes and it brings snow.

Jessica Oertel
Age: 11

The rain slaps the ground,
It glistens in the lightning
The sun will shine again

Tim Brechlin
Age: 12

DEATH

Death comes to me during the day.
Death comes to me during the night.
Death surrounds us all,
   from morning to night,
   night to morning.
God sends this plague
   to punish us for our sins.
Don't sin, be peaceful,
   be simple, be happy,
   help others and you
   may go to Heaven for eternity.
The Devil loves death
   but God hates it.
Please don't sin.
This is your warning.
If you don't take this seriously
   you will be banished from earth
   into the fiery, burning place of Hell.
So live your life wisely
   otherwise you will die
   A SAD man.

Ruchir Narayan
Age: 12

SNOWFLAKES

Whirling,
Twirling,
Very pretty
Only here for awhile --
What a pity.
Here they lay
In their merry way
Each unique in a special way.

I LOVE SNOW!

Natalie Jasien
Age: 10

A leaf of autumn
Plunges from a hollow
tree
And covers summer

Adam Stillo
Age: 12

UNDER MY BED

Under my bed where the fungus grows
I dare NOT put my toes.
For I don't know what's under there;
"OH!" never mind
It's just my...
DIRTY UNDERWEAR!!!!!

Bryan Kett
Age: 10

WOLF

Howling on a cliff
In the light of the moon he
Calls to his gray friends.

Matthew Cleary
Age: 6

EAGLE AT DAWN

I climb to the butte to greet the morning
The sun breaks through the cloud rainbow
Below, wind takes the dust as prisoners
And carries them to the rolling hills
Above me, an eagle soars
Wings outstretched
Cawing at the world below
A feather drops from the never-ending sky.

Rachel Repke
Age: 13

THANKSGIVING

My dog ate Thanksgiving
Turkey and all!
Pass the mashed potatoes
Boy, he used to be small
At first we thought he was having babies
But then we remembered he was a boy
Mother called the doctor
But then we got him a toy
I don't think we can make him thin again
But, we will do our very best
This was just a catastrophe
Well, that's the end

John H. Boumgarden
Age: 10

WOLF CRIES

A family of wolves howl into the dark sky
with the music of the night,
　The dark peaks of the mountains look like fingers
emerging from the ground reaching for the heavens,
　The fresh scent of night rain floats to the ground,
　My cold breath disappears into the darkness,
　The wind rages up my spine with chilling strength
of the night.

Katie Silvia
Age: 13

GOOD-BYE

I couldn't believe it when
You told me you were moving away.
I was left with the smallest
Hope that you'd be back someday.
I know you'll be back to visit,
But it just won't be the same.
I'm gonna miss your laugh and smile
And calling out your name.
In August I'll be on your driveway,
Tears streaming down my face.
Watching your car drive out of sight
I feel so out of place.

Cari Gresh

WATERFALL

The water flows down,
Fish squirming to be unscathed,
Sun glistens upon its rushing sheet,
A rainbow comes to visit.

Jordan Wilson
Age: 12

A LOVELY MORNING

-- Through the eyes of an Indian Maiden --

New wild flowers,
Opening and soaking up the golden rays,
A bird flying through the clear, morning sky,
One lone feather drifted from its body.

The freshly picked and dew-covered berries to eat,
A deep drink from the clear,
Almost mirror image, water.

Seeing the sun setting,
Reds, oranges, pinks, blues, and purples,
A Lovely Morning.

Jennifer Cowart
Age: 13

THE WOLF

The wolf crouches
Its belly scraping against the ground
Waiting for its prey
Its nose twitches
Its breath fogs in the cold night
Waiting for its prey
The weasel runs
The wolf strikes
Like prairie lightning
There is no escape from the prairie grass wolf.

Kurt Fieser
Age: 13

A river flows
To the ocean, an everlasting cycle
Like veins of the globe
Crisscrossing the land

Chris Kartalia
Age: 12

IF TREES COULD TALK

If trees could talk oh what
would they say?
Would they yawn at dawn to
pass the time away?
Would they scream, "Oh no!
I'm losing my leaves!"
While slowly comes that warm
autumn breeze?
Would time fly
as squirrels squirm by?
When the snow trickles down
they might frown.
But soon they will discover
that every tree will soon lose
its cover.
If trees could talk oh what
would they say?
Would they slowly learn to
frolic and play?
Would they talk to friends
like me and you?
Would they play with toys as
children often do?
What would trees say or do
if they could talk like me and
you?

Tabytha Y. Grimm
Age: 12

THE WALK

I walked down the row with the dirt between my toes.
Not knowing where I may go.
The sun beating on me.
The curves and hills before me.
The sparrows following me.
And no where to go but to walk on and on.

With the sun in my eyes and a breeze that lay still.
There's no water near, no people there.
Not a house in sight, just a light.
That seems to shine.
And all I can do is walk on and on.

I seem to get tired but determined I am.
The light seems closer, and the voices seem louder.
I call and call but no one answers.
And all I can do is walk on and on.

Jennifer Mathre
Age: 13

FLYING SOUTH

Flying through the sky,
Trying to keep the dust out of your eye,
Looking back to say good-bye,
To your friends who are very shy.

Mac Barclay
Age: 12

BEST FRIENDS

There's someone you can count on
whenever you are sad.
They're your friends.
You can see them at school
or when you are at home
they're your friends.
If you need them they'll be there.

Dawn Dawson
Age: 12

BASEBALL...MY SPECIAL FRIEND

Baseball is a very great sport,
this I must not retort.
If baseball were a crime,
I'd be doing time.
I like to play at shortstop,
where I rank among the top.
The crowd looks at me in awe,
as I create no flaw.
I dive and jump and throw the ball,
without so much as a little stall.
And here my poem comes to an end,
for baseball is my special friend.

Matt R. Prombo
Age: 12

FISHIN'

Fishin' is very fun
You don't have to work or run
You have to make the precise precisions
You have to make the right decisions
You don't have to have too much muscle
Fishin' isn't a big hustle
You can fish at a real lake
Or at one that is fake
When the big fish comes
It will put up a big fight
It will take a lot of might
Fishin' takes rods and reels
Fishin' brings up many good meals
Finally when the day is over
You will come home to your dog Rover
You will clean and cook your catch up
And feed some to the pup
Then you lay down your head
And you will go right to bed.

Marty Ahrens
Age: 12

MICHAEL JORDAN

Michael Jordan is a great performer
He runs down the court and shoots from the corner
When he gets hit on the arm
The referee blows the alarm
He goes to the line
And makes number nine
The Bulls are leading by ten
And you know they're gonna win again

Luke Thomas
Age: 11

WOLF'S PRAIRIE

Long grass sways in the breeze,
It moves like waves in the ocean.
Shadows, like tall dark soldier, stretching,
reaching out, as the sun sets behind the distant hills.
The sweet smell of prairie grass surrounds me,
The strong mint-like smell of pine trees and
the cool fresh air comforts me.
I can hear the wind whistling in the trees,
as Mother Nature sings her lullaby.
I feel a sudden breeze rush through me,
and then leaving me still in silence.

Janette Dunne
Age: 13

Darkness is a cape over the air.
Though still, it ripples in the breeze.
Suddenly it stops.
All is still and quiet.
I stay in my house and stare
Out of the window and at the night.
A cold universe.
No one is there, yet I see
Everyone.
Wind and sky dance together,
Together they sweeten the sky.
Stars are hiding behind clouds
To come out later,
When no one is up writing poems,
Like I am tonight.
The stars are shy tonight,
Brave on other evenings,
Just like people everywhere.
Nothing is here,
Yet I see much.
Where there is nothing, there is everything.
When you look into the stillness of the night.
The same is true for this poem --
It is titleless,
Without rhythm,
Without rhyme,
Where there is nothing, there is everything.

Cara Donfrio

small and timid, i sit
on my haunches in a corner
watching everything with topaz eyes

my meow is a mere whisper
my purr but a low rumble
as i try to speak

with claws extended, i sit
upon velvet feet in restless anxiety
remembering all with keen insight

too little to be noticed
too young to be taken seriously
i observe my animal world

Theresa Herbst
Age: 17

WITCHES AND GOBLINS

Goblins asked witches,
"Are you witches or switches?"
Witches asked goblins,
"Are you goblins or robins?"
The witches said,
"We are not switches we are witches
and don't switch us again!"
The goblins said,
"Don't worry about us
we just do the robbing around here."

DeAnna Maria Kontos

FRIENDS

A key to a door,
A cap to a marker,
A doll to a dress,
A pair of shoes.

A page to a book,
A button to a coat,
A pair of earrings,
A to B.

A leaf to a tree,
An eraser to a pencil,
A star to the sky,
A label to a can.

A lace to a shoe,
A feather to a bird,
A branch to a tree,
A bead to a necklace.

A fish to a river,
A child to a school,
A hair to a dog,
An eye to a face.

A crayon to a box,
A toy to a shelf,
A magnet to a refrigerator,
My friend and myself!

Ashley Burns
Age: 10

A FLAT GNAT NAMED MATT

Once there was a gnat,
That wasn't skinny and wasn't fat.
The other gnats called him Matt.
One day a cat sat on poor Matt.
Matt wasn't skinny, he wasn't fat
He was flat.
What a brat that cat!

Noah Peter Wiza
Age: 11

JULIE'S JUNKY JUGS

Julie Jordan juggled junky jugs.
Junky jugs Julie Jordon juggled.
If Julie Jordan juggled junky jugs,
Where are the junky jugs Julie Jordon juggled?

Julie Ann Mueller
Age: 10

THE FLY THAT THREW A PIE

There once was a thing called a fly,
who decided to throw a pie,
it hit me,
oo, ow, ee
it hit me right in the eye.

I decided to clean it up,
I decided to use my pup,
she licked it off,
she started to cough,
I gave her water in a cup.

Paul Cowgill
Age: 10

PETTING A DOG

With a stroke of a hand
And a pat on the head
With a little yip
And a little bark
A puppy likes to be petted.
With a stroke of a brush
And a wisp of a comb
The puppy is very soft.
With a slurp and a munch
The puppy is full.

Amanda Tuntland
Age: 11

THEY ARE BUGGING ME

Oh no I see some bees,
Uh oh here comes some fleas.
I hope I don't get any bites,
I think I see some tiny mites.
There I see some ants,
They're crawling up my pants!
There is a ladybug,
She is on my favorite rug!
There is a dragonfly,
"Ow" he bit my poor thigh!
Now there is a gnat,
Sitting on my cute cat.
Then I woke up
It was all just a dream.

Lisette DeDera
Age: 10

LEAVES

L eaves fall when autumn rises.
E veryone likes to jump in a pile of leaves.
A lmost everybody likes when the leaves
   change color.
V iolet, orange, yellow, and red, are the colors
   of the leaves.
E very leaf changes color in fall.
S o many colors in fall.

Michael Anthony DiBrito
Age: 10

FALL LEAVES

L eaves live in trees.
E verybody jumps in leaf piles.
A ll people like to rake leaves.
V ivid tangerine leaves are ready to fall.
E verybody naps after a long day.
S trawberries are fun to eat in the fall.

Mark W. Myatt
Age: 10

L eaves falling off trees
E verywhere you go you see leaves falling
A ll over there's brown leaves
V ery bright color leaves fall
E very kind of leaves fall on trees
S o many leaves falling

Aide Garduno
Age: 11

L eaves are everywhere, in people's backyard.
E veryone is happy that it's fall.
A utumn is my favorite season.
V ery little people are in their houses.
E veryone is raking the leaves.
S o many people like fall.

Bianca Maria Frusa
Age: 11

BASEBALL IS FUN

Baseball is fun
with the hits and homers.
I like baseball for the action
and the great excitement
at every at-bat
and every play.

John Paul Reyns
Age: 11

TERROR TODDLERS

Little kids always break their toys
It's mostly the boys
They make a mess,
but will never confess
They rip the rug in the hall,
and climb up every wall
They break your mom's broom,
and mess up your room
They tear out the shade
and scare the poor maid
They break every piece of glass,
and always complain about going to Mass
They steal your money,
and tease your pet bunny
They jump in every lake and almost drown
They're never happy they always frown
They jump in the leaves your father raked up,
and break your mom's best china cup
They break the lamp shade,
So you won't get your allowance paid
They starve the dog,
and eat like a hog
They tell you a dumb joke,
and put things in your food that will make you choke
They eat your dinner and your food
They're always in a bad mood
If you happen to have in your house a little boy
Then you know, it's not a joy

Bianca Alana Reggi
Age: 10

SPRING

Spring is when the flowers bloom
Spring is when the caterpillars come out
Of their cocoon
Spring is when the birds lay eggs
And the children go outside and play all day.

Meghan Brown
Age: 9

Computers
Big, gray
Flashing screens
Helping me learn everyday
Teachers

Bobbe Padilla
Age: 10

DEER

Deer are very strong,
A deer walks through the forest,
It holds its head high.

Joseph Kowalewski
Age: 8

THE NIGHT

I love to look up at night,
To see the beauty of God's creation,
I love the stars, that give the dark sky
A beautiful white tint,
I love to see the blazing comets
That dash through the sky,
I love to look at the mysterious patterns
The stars create,
I love the giant moon,
That lights a bright hue in the sky
That makes people awe with delight,
That is why I love the night.

James Cotiguala
Age: 10

I KNOW WHEN IT IS AUTUMN WHEN . . .

I know when it is autumn when . . .
The leaves on trees turn bright red and gold.
When the leaves surround you like knights
In shining armor surrounding the dragon.
When jack-o'-lanterns are on every front porch.
When you see animals running this way
And that hunting for food for the long, cold winter.
That is how I know it is autumn.

Geoffrey Schnorr
Age: 10

BUSY BEES

Busy bees, busy bees,
Flit around the leafy green trees,
Gathering nectar,
For King Hectar,
Into the hive,
With nectar they dive,
The bees like to sing,
To the king,
After the run,
When all the work is done,
Busy bees, busy bees,
Have a sleepy night,
After they have worked with all their might.

Carly Campbell
Age: 11

WORDS

A word is just a word
Some unwise people say,
Still I do not see that way.
That thing they call a word
Is the beauty of the earth.
It's the feelings that you feel,
Yes, it's true a word may hurt.
But what cheers you up when you are down
Is those words that people say,
To make you feel that way.
So now I hope you don't think a word
Is just a word.

Katherine C. Powers
Age: 10

HALLOWEEN

Halloween is a spooky day,
Better watch out where you play,
There are ghosts and goblins and witches too,
When they want to scare you they just say BOO!

Watch out when you look behind,
Vampires, skeletons, and monsters, too
All I can say is
"Be careful when you look behind you!!!"

Linda Jean Molloy

HALLOWEEN NIGHT

It's Halloween night,
In the old lady's house,
There's a skeleton in the basement,
And a spider as big as a mouse.
There's a mummy in his tomb,
And a night owl sitting in the moon gloom.
There's a vampire in a coffin and a bloody bat.
Frankenstein's in the bathroom,
Telling a mouse to scat.
And a ghost hiding in the closet,
There's a zombie in the grass,
And a goblin broke the glass.
But the worst thing had to be,
When they all stared at me.

Dylan Wienke
Age: 8

HALLOWEEN NIGHTS

It's night
and all the lights are bright
The costumes glear
with shivering fear
The dogs howl
and there's a hoot from an owl
Boo...

Joey Hanna

RAIN FOREST

Rain forest, rain forest how would it be,
To not have monkeys swing in your trees?

When the tractor comes by to clear all the land,
The animals will cry when they're left with just sand.

Roads will come and houses built too,
Nature and wildlife, lost for the new.

The zoo is a place to remember what was.
The rain forest has died and it's gone just because.

Brian Hutcheson

WINTER

The snowflakes fall
And the trees glitter
The snow is tall
And it is winter.

Kids come and play,
Snowmen are built,
Snow will come again on a new day,
The trees will tilt.

Pavithra Nagarajan
Age: 10

As the sun disappears over the horizon
the air chills.
The birds tuck their heads deep
in their wings to keep warm.
A wolf is howling in the distance.
In the morning the sun shines radiantly.
The leaves change from plain green
to beautiful colors.
As the day rolls on clouds form.
The drizzling of the clouds is refreshing,
And that's an autumn day.

Sara Nawrocki
Age: 10

FOOTBALL

Football is a great sport,
I love football,
The sound of helmets hitting against each other,
Sweat dripping from your head,
Working as a team,
Passing the ball,
Handing off the ball,
Trying to get to the goal line,
And celebrating with your team.

Kevin Flaherty
Age: 10

FALL LEAVES

The leaves turn brown,
They circle 'round and 'round,
They sit in a big pile of leaves,
They fall off of trees.

Jeff Falater
Age: 9

A SUMMER DAY

One day my mouse ran away
while I was fishing by the bay.

When I got home I looked for her,
(funny how my cat did purr...).

So, I looked in the kitchen by the broom,
I saw her as she ran out of the room.

I saw her next to the TV,
but then she started to chase me.

I showed her the fish I caught today,
when I was fishing by the bay.

She said to me, "You keep the fish,
I prefer cheese on a dish."

Mary Dorner
Age: 9

WHERE THE LEAVES DANCE

The leaves dance on the sidewalk
They twist
and are very swift.
They got crumpled
and rumpled
There are no leaves on the sidewalk.
The next day
they got up and danced
and pranced
until they got tired
and went to sleep.

Cole Franzen
Age: 8

FALL

Fall comes but once a year
We aren't happy to see it go
Don't shed a tear
Just because fall comes once a year.
Fall will be back again,
You'll see
Believe me
Don't shed a tear
Because fall comes once a year.

Jill Polanski
Age: 9

THE WINDS CALL FALL

I hear the leaves shake,
And I hear the branches break.
I hear the wind's whistling sound,
All around.
The birds all went away,
Because they couldn't stay.
The leaves make a weird sound,
All of them fell on the ground.
There were a lot of fall showers,
But there were not many flowers.
Summer has gone away,
But it is going to come back another day.

Nicole Papalia
Age: 8

TWISTER

I watched from the window,
As trees flew by,
All I wanted to do was cry.
By dawn it was over,
That was not at all fun,
The twister had come, had seen, had won.

Lesley Chmell
Age: 9

AUTUMN

Trees change their dress to shades
Of orange, red, and gold,
To pave the sidewalks with mosaics to behold
Leaves fall from their trees like raindrops from the sky
Preparing for the long, cold winter ahead
And leaving bare branches behind
The season comes and then it goes
But of one thing you can be sure,
The cycle will begin again
Sometimes early, sometimes late
And its beauty will endure

Jasmine Villanova
Age: 10

FALL

This is the time of year,
When people are full of cheer.
Where leaves fall on the ground,
And the ground can't be found.
People eat turkey and potatoes,
And the table is set for a great big feast!

Alexandra Loken
Age: 9

LEAVES

They're all over the ground.
Oh! They're all around.
They fall from a tree.
That's what I see.

Kyle Wright
Age: 8

My one pet peeve...
Is my first name!

When I get upset,
I have my parents to blame.

I would like to smack
the ones that call me "Jack."

My full name is so long,
That even I spell it wrong.

Another thing about my name, Jackie,
Is that is just so happens to rhyme with wacky.

At least my name is not Priscilla,
because that rhymes with the word . . . gorilla!

Jacqueline Flavin
Age: 10

SUMMER

Warm days,
Children play,

Lots of fun,
In the sun,

Flowers bloom,
Brides of June,

Barbecues,
Swimming pools,

Fireflies,
Fourth of July,

Sand,
Visiting the Rio Grande,

And...
Mosquitoes!

Erin Cathleen Clemens
Age: 10

SNOW

Snow falls in my yard.
It falls cold, heavily, fast, white.
It falls all around.

Adrian Peter Varga
Age: 8

BUMBLEBEES

Bees, bees, bumblebees
Flying in the summer breeze
Flying, flying everywhere
Flying in the cool air

Bees, bees, bumblebees
They make honey for you and me
Making, making honeycombs
In their little beehive homes

Margaret Hejna
Age: 10

SCHOOL IS FUN

Books are fun
But books are done
Books are fun
But my teachers are more fun
Math is fun
But math is done
Math was fun
But my teachers are more fun
P.E. is fun
But P.E. is done
P.E. was fun
But my teachers are morc fun
Work is fun
But work is done
Work was fun
But my teachers are more fun
Music is fun
But music is done
Music was fun
But my teachers are more fun
School is fun
But school is done
School was fun
But my teachers are more fun

Jessica Kveton
Age: 8

WHAT IS LOVE?

What is a home?
A home is a place to depend on.
What is a family?
A family is someone to love.
What is love?
Love is what you feel when you would do anything
    for a person or an animal or a thing.
It is not just another emotion.
There is love in a home.
There is love in a family.
There is love in a little girl's worn-out teddy bear
    with only one eye.
What is a life without love?
Nothing.

Heather Morton
Age: 12

HOW LIFE IS

Everybody says life's simple
even when they get a pimple.
Everybody says life's a breeze
even when they're told to eat their peas.
Everybody says life's a bowl of cherries
not just any berries.
Well, they're all WRONG!

Stephani Pescitelli
Age: 8

THE EAGLE

I was looking at the clouds one day,
Puffy white with specks of gray.
As I watched, a flake of gold,
Interrupted the sky so bold.
I watched him soar with gentle grace
And soon I saw his noble face.
The dark black eyes were as black as coal
And yet they held a gentle soul.
Then as graceful as when he had come,
He swooped back up and was gone.

Many years later I heard a story told
Of a man who was so bold.
I then returned to once more see
The graceful creature that had looked at me.
When I arrived I saw a man
And watched how proud he did stand.
He looked at me with eyes of coal,
And I saw the same gentle soul.
With a puff of smoke the eagle returned
And I, with my lesson learned,
Shared a look that would not end
And I said good-bye to my wild friend.

Rachael Collins
Age: 16

99

My mom is my best friend
There when I need her
I know I can depend
On help from my mother.

My mom is my teacher
I'm learning each day
I know I can reach her
If I go the wrong way

My mom is my guide
Watching over me
She keeps me in line
Everything she does see.

She is loving and kind,
A better Mom, I'll never find!

Anna Staffeldt
Age: 16

MY BUNNY

Boom-Boom is my bunny's name.
Thump, thump, thumping is his game.
He thumps all day.
He thumps all night.
I guess that's just how he plays.

Kaitlin Giles Ii
Age: 8

WISHES

Lying there still under the bright sky.
I'm lying there in a daze,
thinking to myself I'd like to fly.
Some stars are covered by the haze.
Each star has its own purpose,
while others just stay afloat.
Some lie along the surface.
Some stars make a shape of a gigantic boat.
I think it would be fun
to run around the moon.
To stop and have a talk with the sun,
When it is about noon.
I really wish that I can go,
When in reality it's just a show.

Jodi Lyn Stahl
Age: 16

HAVE FUN?

I was fun.
Until I got too much sun.
And then I had to run!
I ran into the water.
And then my brother hit me with a swatter.
Then I went home to bed.

Nikki Christensen
Age: 8

CRIME

If you're gonna talk the talk,
then walk the walk.
If you're gonna do the crime,
then pay the time.
Crimes these days is all you hear,
like doing marijuana and drinking beer.
On the news it's all bad.
It's really sad when people kill.
They don't even do it against their will.
Some people drink and drive.
And sadly they don't stay alive.
So just remember, if you do the crime,
pay the time.

Jenna Kylene King
Age: 12

ANGELA

A lways moving
N ever stopping
G ood at softball
E verlasting energy
L oving
A nd caring

Angela Rogde
Age: 11

IMAGINE...

Imagine the place you live in
Isn't where you want to be.

Imagine the person you are inside
Isn't who you want to be.

The struggle of everyday life
Is shared by everyone you see.

And the struggle to escape
Is rarely but a dream.

Imagine for a second...
If it were me who finally escaped.

Imagine for a second...
It was more than just a dream.

Where would i go?
Who would i be?

The only place i know
The only place i've been.

My own house
House on Mango Street.

Ayesha Atique
Age: 16

AS I LAY THEE DOWN TO SLEEP...

I look at this child,
So warm and mild,
As he stares up at me,
I see,
my future,
Me as a mother,
looking down I think,
with a wink,
I lay my lips against his forehead,
And like I said,
As I put this child to bed,
His eyes gently roll into his head,
Good night my love good night!

Amanda Gagliani
Age: 13

SUN

I see you in the east
I see you in the west
When I see your bright colors
It really takes me in

I see you every day that I live
And always will for the rest of my life

Chris Lowery
Age: 11

THE SUN

The beauty of the sunrise
Is something to behold
Glowing like a child's eyes
Seeing joys that are untold
At midday, the sun glares down
Like someone with much hate
To stop the burning gaze,
We only have to wait
At the end of the day
The sun, with sleepy glow
Trudging slowly, as is its way
Like a tired child, just so
Ready to rise again, lighting up today

Rich Pallardy, Jr.
Age: 13

TWISTERS

Sleek as cats;
Gray as mice, roaring like lions,
Down they creep on unexpected prey,
and what we do is pay.
A rope is dropped like God's finger,
and on the ground all it does is linger.
Death and destruction is what it leaves behind
and turns everything into a bind.

Jean Bittner
Age: 14

FALL

It's tons of fun to jump in the leaves.
And fall and call in the leaves.
Oh how fun to jump and bump in the leaves.

Carrie L. Pallardy
Age: 6

THE CAT WENT TO SCHOOL

The Cat went to school.
He saw his friend Bat.
Bat and Cat did math together.
Cat and Bat ate lunch together.
Cat and Bat played outside.
Then they went home on the bus.

Michael Moody
Age: 8

SADNESS

Sadness,
Sadness overcomes me,
Through every slick vein,
Oh, the sorrow that has fallen upon me,
If only I could overcome the rumbling pain,
The pain of depression,
I sit here now grieving,
Grieving because of a broken heart,
A heart which was crushed through the battle of love,
A battle in which I was demolished and destroyed,
But hopefully over a decade of time,
The cracks in my heart will heal,
And I will regain my purity and hope,
I shall stop wandering,
And find the one,
Sadness

Hytham Kilani
Age: 13

THE MOOSE

The moose, the moose
That moose is hiding somewhere.
My pal is lost
Somewhere, somewhere.
He's that moose.

Matthew Novak
Age: 8

OUT WORLD

Drugs, guns, violence, and hate
This is my world up to date
The earth is just a rolling ball
It's the people that make society fall
In your life you look to the stars
Stopped by barriers; enclosed by bars
Walk to the sun; sing to the moon
Life is an act with curtains falling too soon
You fear the future and run from the past
Run forever; your life will not last
Life without direction is life not at all
You will not rise, but only fall
Run for life dive for death
Never knowing if this will be your last breath
Waiting for the clouds of Heaven to come
For someone's life is finally done
Your dreams, wishes, and fantasies
Can never become realities
We live in a world told not to try
Where tears turn to dust but do not dry

Mike Hatchell
Age: 13

Hello! My name is Jeremy Joe.
I like to play with Play-Doh .
I like to listen to the radio.
Mommy lets me watch a game show.
I never ate a Sloppy Joe.

Jeremy Pappalardo
Age: 8

TREE BLUES

Oh, I've got the blues
And red and orange and all colors of autumn
Oh I've got the blues
Because I'm a tree and my leaves are falling.

Ooh winter is a' comin'
And I'm left stark bare and naked
Oh winter is a' comin'
And I'm left without care.

So I've got the blues,
and I'm in despair.

Oh I've got the blues
That no other tree can have
Another leaf is fallin'
And that just makes me more sad.

Annie Royston
Age: 11

THE SEA BY THE BEACH

The sea is blue.
The seaweed is green.
The rocks are gray.
It is nice.
It is sunny.

Luke Campillo
Age: 7

MY T-SHIRT

My T-shirt is all worn out
When my mother saw it she started to shout
"The collar is torn,
The sleeves are all worn,
The front of it is all covered with dirt,
I think you need a brand new shirt!"

Katie M. Hay
Age: 8

110

GENTLY CRYING

I see it falling slowly and gently,
Like a crying child's tears,
Washing away its hurt and pain
As it pedals down to the earth,
Making it clean and fresh again.
I see it as I look out the window on a rainy day,
Trying to ignore the reflection,
I long to take off my shoes
And dance in the rain.
Pedalling rain hits the roof
In its own song of dance,
The sound lolling me to sleep.
As I sleep, I dream of the falling rain
Outside of my window
Reminding me of a crying child's tears
Falling slowly and gently.

Stephanie Kraner
Age: 15

I grew some grass just for you, so you could mow it.
I grew some flowers just for you,
So you could smell them.
I grew a tree just for you, so you could read under it.
I grew some cornstalks just for you,
So you could pick the corn.
I grew some bushes just for you,
So you could look at them.

Jon Ross
Age: 8

THANKFULNESS

Dear Lord,
  We thank you Lord for your gifts to us
We thank you Lord for dying on the cross
We thank you Lord for forgiving our sins
We thank you Lord for the trees and moss
We thank you Lord for the nature and wind
We really want to thank you Lord
We really want to bless your name
Hallelujah you are our King.

Lindsey Anderson
Age: 11

I went to my house
What did I see?
Food!
I went to my house
What did I see?
My friend!
I went to the park
What did I see?
A black cat!
I went to a house
What did I see?
A ghost!

Scott Stehlin
Age: 9

There was a frog
who sat on a log
He was hungry
but was not grumpy

Kim Wiltjer
Age: 10

THIRD GRADE

Third grade can be fun
But there are days you just want to run.
Every morning the bell does ring
There are days I just want to sing.
Now my day is ready to end
Some teacher is happy again.

Eric Benjamin Mann
Age: 10

SEASONS CHANGE

He said nothing changes,
  it all stays the same.
The next year I went there,
  but he never came.
When I went home, I got a letter.
He said he found a new girl ,said she was
    better.
Said she had eyes like the blue of the
    sea.
My eyes are brown, huh lucky me.
He said he was sorry for all he had done,
said the laughter was great,
  and the phone calls were fun.
As I sat in my dark room alone,
I thought how I should have been smarter,
  I should have known.
that nothing lasts forever, it all goes away,
then I'm the one who has to pay.
As I write this poem, my mind will
  wonder,
Will I ever love again,
  I must ponder.

Ali Tannenbaum
Age: 13

DAWN

Standing at the ocean's edge
the sun rises at your feet
painting indigo canvas skies
with the fiery orange of dawn

Pearl white stars are
still shining up above
in a last vestige of midnight
in a far corner of the sky.

Waves caress your bare feet
sliding the velvet softness
of fine watery sand to fit
like a glove around your heels

High above you
night is falling
Deepest black becomes inky blue
and turns to the purple of royalty

...you raise your eyes to greet the morning.

Matt Beran
Age: 16

HAWK

KAWWAA is the sound I make,
Every morning as I wake.
Flying through the morning air,
I look around everywhere.
I see my home upon the trees,
And I see something that makes me pleased.
My night is through,
The sun has come.
And just in time my poem is done!

Daniel Schaffer

MEMORIES

The years have passed with sorrow and shame.
Memories fall into my head like leaves fall off a tree.
The river of life comes up like a tide.
Steady at first,
but rippling with pain.
I say I am strong,
but my weakness is coming.
Striking my heart like a bolt of lightning.
Then at last I am free,
but sadness will come soon to beat me.

Belinda Manly
Age: 13

If only life was as easy as pie
maybe so many people wouldn't die

We constantly place our troubles
on outlooks of bubbles

Maybe life wouldn't be so hard
if you listened
To small voices that say
stop

And then when all can do that
maybe so many people wouldn't strike-out at bat

That is all I have to say
so I leave you with this, okay

Life is good, life is great
live it so that when you die
you don't have to worry about
what people say.

Juliet E. May

COME, OH BRAVE VETERANS

Oh, you wonderful Veterans,
I remember unpleasant times,
When you left me behind,
left your homes and your lives,
to fight for our country and pride,
with guns and knives.

I shall say no more.
We must make peace,
with Germans, Asians, and Russians,
We must make peace with all.

This has gone on long enough,
I know the troubles of war.
I know that you are hurt,
for I am hurt, too.

Come to me.
You once took care of me,
giving up your young lives,
so I could live safely.
It is my turn now, to care for you.

I will cure your wounds,
your pains of war,
and soften your memories.
Come to me.

You risked your lives,
to keep me secure
I want to keep you secure now.
Come.

The words of war are old,
You know that.
You mustn't think of defeat,
it's an old word.
Shame isn't new either.

Come to me.
I will show you that you are heroes.

Come,
Oh Brave Veterans.
Come to me,
I know you're there,
full of pride.

Come to me.
I will soften your memories of war,
and celebrate your return.

Come,
Oh brave Veterans,
come to me, Miss Liberty,
on this
VETERAN'S DAY!!

Neelima Vidula
Age: 10

TWISTER

Once there was a twister
in New York.
The twister twisted up the city
like a massive-sized fork.

Ryan Clausen
Age: 10

When a pig,
Ate a twig,
It gave a yell
A great big yell,
He jumped up high,
Into the sky,
On the Fourth of July

With my hand,
I clapped with the band,
They played so good
We were in a great mood
When the animals show
I'll tape on video
As they move
They'll prove
They're the best
Better than the rest

Karen Kong
Age: 9

SIX FLAGS ADVENTURE

We went to Six Flags
to have a lot of fun.
We rode the Demon four times
and then we were done.

We rented "Rusty but Trusty"
that was our mistake.
We saw a puddle of green liquid
that was not at all fake.

The radiator had leaked
and made a big puddle.
We went to a gas station
that was so cold we had to cuddle.

My mom called my dad
he said he'd be four hours.
so we were stuck in Gurnee
with no showers.

He finally came
at ten.
Others had wondered
where we had been.

Joshua Ryan
Age: 10

SPECIAL THINGS

As I sit and wonder
about the stars, sun, and moon,
I think of happy times,
like a summer afternoon.

Those clouds so white and fluffy,
the sun is shining bright,
but nothing could be better
than a cold winter night.

Sipping my hot chocolate,
watching the fire,
I also love it when
the animals go into shelter.

The leaves fall off the trees
and the air becomes so cool.
The only thing better is when
the flowers start to bloom.

Baby animals everywhere,
they all start to appear.
Nothing makes me happier,
than knowing someone cares.

Lying in my bed each night,
I know that someone's there.
Watching over me from
high up in the air.

All these things are
the ones that
make life
easier to bear.

Melissa Jung
Age: 12

AMONG THE HORIZON

I am a wolf who sits on a high hill in the prairie,
I watch the yellow, purple, and orange sunset,
I notice the grass sways from the wind,
Dirt blows past my face,
The night bugs buzz in my ears,
The air feels like a sheet of silk
That glides around the earth,
I can smell peacefulness,
In the natural prairie.

Laura Kozon
Age: 12

Bert Bear boasted about,
Beating Barney Bird,
At basketball before breakfast.

Katie Gustafson
Age: 10

I AM

I am someone who cares about all people.
I wonder about my future.
I hear cries all around the world.
I see dying on the streets.
I want to see a change in the world.
I am a good friend to family and friends.

I pretend to be a teacher after school.
I feel afraid of violence that hurts others.
It touches my heart when something is wrong.
I worry about kids killing other kids.
I cry when someone close to me dies.
I am a special person to everyone.

I understand about the sadness in the world.
I say "Everything will be okay."
I dream for blacks and whites to be friends.
I try to do my best in everything.
I hope to get married one day and have kids.
I am a caring person to all people.

Nantesha Banks
Age: 12

FIRST IMPRESSIONS

I saw two houses along the riverbank,
One standing proud with courage
far in the stinging blue sky.
The other house was stooping down,
drunk with low self-esteem.

The first house had nicely groomed grass
with no weeds in it,
shiny, glossy windows,
and, with a freshly paved driveway,
one velvet convertible,
waxed and shiny in the burning radish sunset.

In the vision of my eyes,
I say the house that could, that would,
just wreck someone's soul.
There it stood,
short and with slumped-over shoulders,
with a shaggy roof, somewhat like a flickering candle
getting ready to burn out on a December night.
Its supports rotted like an apple in the sun.

Although both very different,
I do recall something alike:
the way they make me feel,
warm inside, with great joy.
Two houses I saw.

Quiton Hoskins
Age: 11

DREAMS

I dream about lots of things,
  about friends, family, people and school.
I dream about lots of things,
  sometimes I have nightmares
  being scared, alone, and even lost.
I dream about lots of things,
  not every dream is great
  sometimes a friend dies,
  or I have a bike wreck
  or something like that,
  but they're not even close
  to being nightmares.
I dream about lots of things,
  Maybe I'm a millionaire, or very poor,
  or won twenty million in the lotto,
  or about last night's date.
I dream about lots of things,
  I sometimes dream about being the president
  or having my own country
  or how about my own basketball shoe.
I dream about lots of things,
  I dream about a thousand dollar allowance
  or my own Harrier jet
  or how about a world record.
I dream about lots of things,
  Yet all of these are dreams and maybe,
  just maybe, they'll be realities
  and if I try they could be.
  Otherwise, they're just dreams
  that I'll never have.
  But as far as I know

dreams are fantasies
that we wished we'd have.

Dylan Jeffries
Age: 13

CHRISTMAS

Christmas is a day of joy.
When you get a toy.
It is a day of play.
It is cold in the winter snow.
So I stay away.
I stay in the house with my little toy mouse.
And eat my Christmas dinner.

Lauren Lipine
Age: 9

RED SCENTS

I was in the garden,
eating apples, raspberries,
strawberries, and cranberries,
drinking Coca-Cola,
with no one around,
in a Bull's uniform,
I was very happy, so I smelt a rose.

Amber Cox
Age: 10

PURPLE

Purple feels like a soft blanket.
Purple sounds like the gentle breeze.
Purple tastes like a sweet sugar plum.
Purple smells like a light perfume.

Heather Mershon
Age: 10

A MOUSE IN THE HOUSE

My cat, she caught a mouse
She brought it in the house
It was still alive, and ran away
Until I caught it on a tray
I put it by the garden gate
And then I told my cat "You're great!"

Amber M. Dillavou
Age: 11

YELLOW

Yellow feels like the vibration in a thunderstorm
Yellow looks like lightning in a hurricane
Yellow is the grass in the prairie
Yellow is lemonade in the summer

David Strathman
Age: 10

BLUE

Blue is like a hot summer sky
At midnight when owls are awake
Sometimes you can taste it in a snowflake
Blue smells like a blueberry jelly donut.

Alicia A. Miner
Age: 10

I hear...
Fast wind blowing on Christmas Eve
Having boys and girls running around in the snow
With trees in the way of each other
I feel snow drifting on people's faces.

Ben Powers
Age: 10

COLOR

Green reminds me of a calm spring day,
As I take a look around
I see many different colors
In birds and other plants, and animals,
As my dad calls me in for dinner,
I turn around and think about the colors I saw.

Kyle C. Thomas
Age: 19

THE ROSE

Looking at the rose
all round, red, and bright
holding it in my hand
wishing it could be in light.

Kelly Dalton
Age: 10

PURPLE

purple feels like strong wind
purple sounds like grapes being picked off a vine
purple taste like fresh picked grapes
purple smells like grape jelly.

Rhiannon Konitski
Age: 10

STORM

It sounds like thunder,
It feels like a storm is coming,
It tastes like a salty ocean,
I can hear the wind humming.

Ashley Wiles
Age: 11

THE COLOR BLUE

Blue feels like a cozy pillow
It sounds like a breeze on a cold winter day
Blue tastes like a juicy watermelon
The best thing about the color blue is that,
It smells like a hot cup of cocoa

Elizabeth M. Meyers
Age: 10

THE WIND

It blows near my window
and reminds me of the past.
It will stay out there forever
and makes sure I finish last.
It calls my name in my deepest slumber
and it waits for me to awake.
I cry out for mercy, asking it, "Why?,"
for my soul's the one at stake.
It stays out there and laughs at me,
making the tears roll down my eyes.
It slaps its harshness across my face,
and ignores my pleading cries.
It knows my pain forth and back,
and it knows I haven't the strength
to return the attack.
I'm like a feather,
riding on its menacing knee.
For it knows I can never take its control away from me.
I don't know where I'm going,
and I don't know where I've been.
All I know is that soon, like others,
I'll also be gone with the wind.

Diana Wallens
Age: 13

I AM

I am a model student.
I wonder about being a police officer.
I hear trouble in school.
I see people everywhere I go.
I want money so I can buy the things I need.
I am a model student.

I pretend I am myself.
I feel good about my birthdays.
I touch my roller blades
When I put them on after school.
I worry about scary noises.
I cry when I need to.
I am a model student.

I understand everything in reading class.
I say, "Why me?," when something bad happens.
I dream about passing fifth grade.
I try to do everything I possibly can.
I hope for peace in life.
I am a model student.

Parish Cameron
Age: 11

I AM

I am a big brother of a little boy.
I wonder what he will be doing in six years.
I hear when he is hurt outside of school.
I see him hurt himself playing.
I want him to have a happy life.
I am a big brother of a little boy.

I pretend to see someone else,
But I see my little brother.
I feel his pain when he cries.
I touch all the sores on his body.
I worry if he is hurt very badly.
I cry if he is hurt at times.
I am a big brother of a little boy.

I understand when he cries at times.
I say "What is wrong with you?"
I dream for him to be happy.
I try to be a good big brother for him.
I hope he will be happy forever.
I am a big brother of a little boy.

James Johnson
Age: 11

CHRISTMAS TREE

Green
Tall
Tree
Angel
Star
Ornaments
Pine needles
Smells like pine
Evergreen
Stem

Ashley M. Overcash
Age: 8

The music made me so happy
That I wanted to dance
On the way to church
My family and I started to prance
As I stood with my family
In the church lobby
I started to get unhappy
Thinking of my cousin Robbie
Though he's been gone many years
It still brings real tears.
As the music got slow
It started to snow!

Samantha Spring
Age: 10

TERROR

Terror is black!
It tastes like green spinach.
It smells like garbage in a landfill
And reminds me of burnt pizza.
It sounds like screaming in a haunted house,
Terror makes me feel like hiding under the bed!

Justin Brown
Age: 8

SOCCER

I love soccer
Soccer is my heart
When I get the ball,
I score off the chart!

Molly Hodges
Age: 11

HALLOWEEN

Halloween is a scary night.
Jack-o'-lanterns shine bright.
You knock on a door and say trick-or-treat.
But it is a mystery you won't know who you meet.
Cats scream with fright.
Benjamin with his kite.
Not a friendly one in sight.
So confusing you won't know what is right.
Where is home? You are lost.
It's getting cold, there is some frost.
There is a monster oozing green.
And a sock not very clean.
I'm getting tired in the alley.
Heading towards the dark valley.
Waiting for your family car.
Hoping it's not very far.
When I get home I will go right to sleep.
I probably won't, I will count sheep.
By the faces you will be petrified.
By the sounds you will be terrified.
When you are hurt you groan and moan.
Hurt your leg or broke a bone.
It's not ABC's or 123's.
Or being chased by a swarm of bees.
It's a scary night on Halloween.
You have to be very keen.
You look up in the sky there are seven black bats.
You look down on the ground there are seven black cats.
You are at home not turned into a bean.
But that was just a dream.
What will you do?
What will you say?

You are confused
because Halloween is not a day to play.
You love candy!! You have six or seven pounds.
The next house has a bunch of hounds
You dare yourself to enter there.
Because all they want to do is rip and tear.
All of a sudden a ghostly man steps on the porch.
And lights a cigar that looks like a torch.
He looked at me with such wonder and stare.
A look that would make someone feel that he didn't care.
It looked like he had a lot of scars on his face.
And his house did not look very nice.
Holding a cup he said something, I heard loud and clear.
And all what he said was why are you here?
In front of my eyes I saw him disappear.
I looked at him and wished I wasn't born.
But then I heard a loud car horn.
I was so happy to know I was going home.
Even though I wanted to go farther, like Paris or Rome!
I'm at home happy to be a teen.

But then again what about next Halloween!!!

Mina Saeed
Age: 9

MY FRIEND

My friend is not like a normal kid,
he's a little different from them all.
We like the same sports and games,
like me his favorite game is ball.
We race and play all over the park,
when I call his name he starts to bark.
You've probably guessed he is not a fish,
bird, or even a frog...
He is just my best friend,
He
is
my
dog.

Robert Ullrich
Age: 10

I WISH

I wish the world was a better place.
I wish people didn't make fun of other people's face.
I wish God's star would start shining on me.
I wish war could stop, and we can let silence be.
I wish people could care about polluting the air.
I wish Jesus could take me to Heaven above,
like a sharing and caring little white dove.
I wish, I wish upon a star very, very, very far.

Ekejirho Oji
Age: 10

HOME SWEET HOME

Home, flowers, grass, cozy,
Nice, warm, loving, big, pretty,
A place to go home, a garden, cool!
A family, beds, always there for you,
Moms.

Julia Field
Age: 8

MY GARDEN

Outside in my garden,
I find such a delight,
There's no place that I'd rather be,
And if a friend should hope to visit,
That's perfectly all right with me!

Erica Colombi
Age: 10

TERROR

Terror is black,
It tastes like burnt pizza!
It smells like rotten cheese
And reminds me of fire!
It sounds like screaming!
Terror makes me feel like lightning is striking me!

Amanda R. Finley
Age: 8

JOY

Joy is light pink,
It tastes like pizza from Pizza Hut.
It smells like beautiful, bright red roses
And reminds me of my mom and dad.
It sounds like a beautiful, peaceful song.
Joy makes me feel like singing and dancing!

Erica Lazzerini
Age: 8

FEAR

Fear is dark black,
It tastes like liver and onion and spinach.
It smells like smoke coming from a house
And reminds me of a robber in my home.
It sounds like screaming in the night.
Fear makes me feel like our fire alarm going off!

Allison Hess
Age: 8

SLEEPINESS

Sleepiness is dark yellow,
It tastes like lime candy.
It smells like chocolate fudge,
And reminds me of whirling wind, swirling around.
It sounds like wind chimes whistling.
Sleepiness makes me feel like I am in a dream.

John Sundstrom
Age: 9

Snowman
frost
snow
falling down
people make snowballs
cold and white

Stuart Wortman
Age: 8

Christmas trees are green
Jesus was born on Christmas
and you get lots of presents,
buy a fat tree.
you sing Christmas carols in front of it,
Santa comes and puts presents around it
Green and red things and decorations all around you.

Kari Johnson
Age: 8

WIND

Trees sway gracefully.
As wind blows leaves on the ground.
You cannot see wind.

Dean Weber
Age: 8

BEAVER

Cute
swims in water
furry
small
funny paws
eats fish

Paul Stanford
Age: 8

Trees are fat
trees are skinny
trees are tall
trees are small
most trees are green
some are in the woods

Jeffrey Weberg
Age: 9

THE SANDY BAND

By a sandy seashore,
The sea plays the symbols.
It is music to my ears,
The rocks hitting each other,
And the sea gulls singing,
It is a Sunday orchestra.

Josh Schinzer
Age: 11

SOCCER GAME

We were up by four,
hoping to score more.
We were running
out of strength,
the field
was gaining length.
We won over all
and what do you know...

I DIDN'T FALL!

Larissa Rudnicki
Age: 10

HAPPINESS

Happiness is bright red!
It tastes like cheese pizza.
It smells like bubble gum
And reminds me of soft music.
It sounds like people singing happy songs!
Happiness makes me feel like jumping
On a huge trampoline!

Jessica White
Age: 8

NATURE'S WONDERS

I like the dodo bird that disappeared a long time ago.
I also like the white tigers, the gazelle's deadly foe.

I wish I had a tank of piranhas
and a brightly colored tropical bird from the Bahamas.

I like poison dart frogs,
and the poisonous snakes you find in swampy bogs.

I like mountains, hills, deserts, and trees
and the Arctic Canada with its cold freeze.

We must respect rain, snow, and thunder,
and every single special wonder.

Carla Michelle Towns
Age: 9

RED

Red is the color of an apple when you take an apple
from the bag.
A jacket is as shiny as an apple when you take it
out of a bag.
A shirt is as red as a jacket.

Rose Schiro
Age: 10

SPRING

Spring has flowers
that twinkle and sway.
That shine in the sunlight
on a bright spring day.
And have blossoms on trees
especially in the month of May.
If you like the color
of the blossoms and birds,
then you should like spring,
because it brings out
the best in every living thing.

Kelly Marie Veroni
Age: 9

SURPRISE

Surprise is bright purple,
It tastes like chocolate chip ice cream.
It smells like a sunny day
And reminds me of my birthday party.
It sounds like a dark, blue sea.
Surprise makes me feel happy like
When I ride my bike with friends!

Max Pickering

SUMMER

Summer is vicious
Comes with a lion's anger
Very fiery hot!

Anders Pauley
Age: 9

GLASSES

Glasses
big
small
any shape
any color
helps you see well
make you look smarter
safety glasses have sides

Kristen Glenn
Age: 8

DOGS

funny
cute
floppy ears
long tails
fun to play with
some big some small
different colors

Benjamin Fabri
Age: 8

TEDDY BEARS

Teddies are so sweet and cuddly
and that is why I think that you should
get a teddy and bring it with you
when you go to beddy.

Allie Clinite
Age: 9

Pine trees
Christmas trees
shiny green
straight and tall
sharp needles
a good decoration
fun to see

Logan Schultz
Age: 8

SEASONS

Spring is when the flowers blossom.
Summer is hot, but cheery.
Fall is a pretty season.
Winter is jolly fun.

Now, tell me which season you like the best.

Sarah Perrine
Age: 9

DEEP TROUBLE

The house is dirty
because of my feet.
The dog is wet
because of my drink.
My mom is mad
because of me
I know I shouldn't
have kicked her in the knee.

Allison Marcon
Age: 9

LIGHTNING

On a stormy night lightning lights up the sky.
It comes right after its enemy thunder.
When the power goes out and you need to go out
Watch out for electricity in the sky.

This brilliant neon light, lights up the sky
On a dark night.
But, beware don't go outdoor or you might be struck
By the dangerous, vicious lightning.

Michael Ryan Rayburn
Age: 10

Snowmen are made of snow.
When snow falls, build a snowman.
Make three big balls.
Stack them up on top of each other and put eyes on it.
Put a hat on it and a mouth.
Put a nose and buttons on it.

Kevin Kilroy
Age: 9

A POLLUTED RIVER

I went to the river --
And I reached down deep,
I pulled out a shoe
And a tire from a Jeep,
I pulled out a desk
And an orange box of clay
And said, "Pick up this river
So all animals can play!"

Phillip Williams
Age: 9

ANGER

Anger is red!
It tastes like fizzling pop.
It smells like gray smoke
And reminds me of madness.
It sounds like me screaming loudly!
Anger makes me feel like
I am pushing someone hard!

Catherine J. Minnaert
Age: 8

WHITE

White feels like a feather
rubbing gently against my skin.
White is the light ring
of silent bells.
White milk
and cookies.
White is the smell
of perfume in Heaven.

Monica Shaw
Age: 11

GUESS WHO

Who is in your bedroom late at night?
Here are some clues.
They are lovable and huggable.
You love to cuddle them.
Some have names others don't.
Anyway they still are cute.
Who is it...
It's a teddy bear.

Brooke Elliott
Age: 10

MUSIC

Music makes me feel good after a bad day.
Music makes me think of a time
Where nothing goes wrong and it's perfect all day.
Music makes me think of perfect weather.
Music gives me courage to do anything.
Music gives me hope to go through each day
Of my life and to face my problems and fears.
That's what music does to me.

Jordan Wayman
Age: 10

GOD

God is with you
Ne'er forget
He is true
Can't be met
He is powerful
He is strong
So be thankful
All day long

Megan Buckman
Age: 11

HALLOWEEN GHOSTS

Halloween is a very scary night.
It is when all the ghosts are in sight.
They fly around all day
Scaring everyone away!!!
A haunted house is a ghost's home.
It is where a ghost roams.
That is all I have to say about ghosts.

Sean Thompson
Age: 9

MYSELF

I'm four foot eight, I'm really cool.
I'm a brain whiz in school.
When I come home I'm really goofy.
I wear shorts when it's below fifty.
My brother thinks I'm his hero
Because I saved a cat last week
But now my brother thinks I'm a geek.
I really love to read.
My friends hate to.
At Halloween my favorite saying is BOO!

Cindy Benik
Age: 8

Twigs are on the ground.
From a tall tree far above.
They come falling down.

Alex Carlson
Age: 9

GRASS

Grass waves in the wind.
Grass has a friend called dirt.
Grass hates being mowed.

Brian Boucek
Age: 9

Hearts are red pink and purple
they bring happiness to the room
they are good valentines that fill hearts with joy.

Kristyn Klint
Age: 8

SPRING

A bird flies by you
A squirrel sits on a bench
Worms crawl around. Spring!

Benjamin Ganz Edwards
Age: 9

HOUSE

Home, room, TV, basement,
backyard, kitchen,
toys, doors, refrigerator, windows,
food, roof, chimney
parents, kids, for sale
food, roof, chimney

Aaron Hopson
Age: 8

Hear the pitter-patter of the hooves
Santa's sleigh is coming nearer and nearer
House after housetop
It goes around and the jingle of Santa is here

Graham Hill
Age: 8

Fall is a season
Leaves are falling and blowing
So have a great time

Andy Pearson
Age: 8

Leaves are falling down.
Light breeze flowing through the air.
And the leaves are swirling.

Peter Junor
Age: 8

The leaves are falling
And winter is approaching
With breezes so cold

Katie Szewczyk
Age: 8

CHEETAH

Has spots and eats meat.
Running fast and runs alone.
Cheetahs climb the trees.

Nicholas Rinaldi
Age: 8

COOKIES

When I walk into the kitchen,
I smell my mom cooking cookies,
And when they're done,
They're very good looking!

Amber Messink
Age: 10

MY MOM

My mom is a rose from the garden of knowledge,
so very rare so sweet as bright
as a blossom as sweet as a plum.

Will Earlywine
Age: 10

BENNY BEAR

Benny Bear, blueberry bubble fish
Blueberry bubble fish, scared Benny Bear
Brown Benny Bear, turned BLUE!!!

Sarah Faerber
Age: 10

VARNAK

Varnak is yellow
Like a quick strike of lightning
In the season of summer
In the dark black sky.

Mallory James
Age: 10

THE AROMA OF CHOCOLATE

Chocolate is the aroma of sweet hot cocoa,
Simmering on the stove of a log cabin,
It makes you feel warm inside.

Cassy Sallee
Age: 10

White roses are sweet
Blue jays are cute
And gardens are nice
And so are you!

Danny Cahill
Age: 8

Mommy, Mommy I am sick,
Mommy, Mommy I am fine,
Mommy, Mommy I love you!
Mommy, Mommy can we go shopping.

Rebecca Jungman
Age: 8

SNOW

Snow is white and cold,
I like to make a snowman,
Snow is nice and soft.

Ann Marie Manzoeillo
Age: 8

The ghost is scary,
The cat is hairy!

Alex Bohn
Age: 7

SQUIRRELS

Squirrels live in trees.
Squirrels make nests with dry leaves
Squirrels drink water

Clayton Ballerine
Age: 8

Thanksgiving
cranberries, turkey
giving, eating, thanking
happy, joyful, hungry, rowdy
Thanksgiving

Jane Knoche
Age: 10

Thanksgiving
giving season
eating thanking laughing
joyful sharing playing giggling
Thankful

Lauren Teune
Age: 10

Turkey
brown, tasty
eating, tasting, filling
hungry, happy, thankful, grateful
Turkey

Christopher Duncan
Age: 11

The brilliant white light.
The tremendous heat of the fire.
The hot orange ashes.

Keith Hamill
Age: 12

Thanksgiving
season, fall
stuffing, cooking, eating
glad, proud, excited, tired
Thanksgiving

Arben Memed
Age: 10

A huge wave hit me
like a towering boulder
from the angry sea.

Nicholas Alexenko
Age: 12

Stars, moons, and the sun
What do they have in common?
They're all in the sky

Katie Kerr
Age: 12

BLUEBIRD

Alice is my pet.
When I walk she flies with me
To the park. She sings.

Erin Mortimer
Age: 5

RAINDROP

A single raindrop
Tumbling through the crisp spring air,
Landing on my shoe.

Stef Milczarek
Age: 12